THIS CANDLEWICK BOOK BELONGS TO:

There are more than 150 different
kinds of octopuses, and the Giant
octopus is the biggest—the tentacles
of the largest one ever found
were an amazing 15¾ feet long!

Even though they are so huge,
Giant octopuses do not attack humans.
They live in coastal waters in the
north Pacific Ocean, and feed mainly
on crabs, clams, and sea snails.

Female Giant octopuses lay eggs
only once in their lives.
They are believed to eat little
or nothing after mating.
Once their eggs have hatched,
female octopuses die.

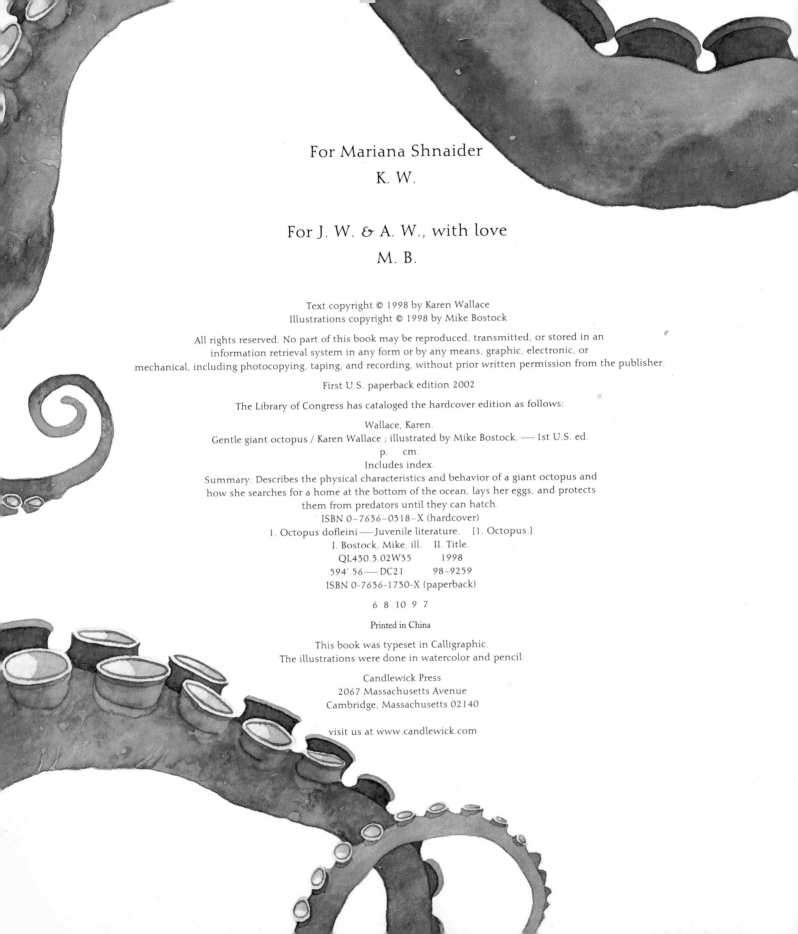

For Mariana Shnaider
K. W.

For J. W. & A. W., with love
M. B.

Text copyright © 1998 by Karen Wallace
Illustrations copyright © 1998 by Mike Bostock

First U.S. paperback edition 2002

The Library of Congress has cataloged the hardcover edition as follows:

Wallace, Karen.
Gentle giant octopus / Karen Wallace ; illustrated by Mike Bostock. — 1st U.S. ed.
p.   cm.
Includes index.
Summary: Describes the physical characteristics and behavior of a giant octopus and how she searches for a home at the bottom of the ocean, lays her eggs, and protects them from predators until they can hatch.
ISBN 0-7636-0318-X (hardcover)
1. Octopus dofleini — Juvenile literature.   [1. Octopus.]
I. Bostock, Mike, ill.   II. Title.
QL430.3.02W35   1998
594'.56 — DC21   98-9259
ISBN 0-7636-1730-X (paperback)

6 8 10 9 7

Printed in China

This book was typeset in Calligraphic.
The illustrations were done in watercolor and pencil.

Candlewick Press
2067 Massachusetts Avenue
Cambridge, Massachusetts 02140

visit us at www.candlewick.com

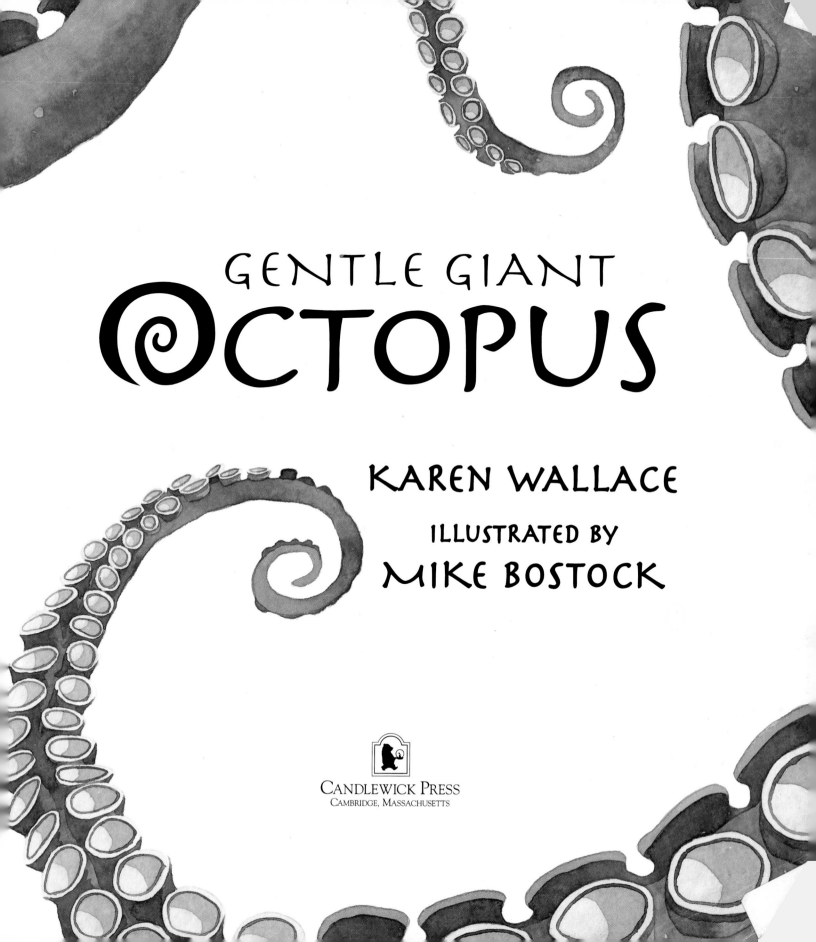

GENTLE GIANT
OCTOPUS

KAREN WALLACE

ILLUSTRATED BY
MIKE BOSTOCK

CANDLEWICK PRESS
CAMBRIDGE, MASSACHUSETTS

A gentle Giant octopus
jets through the shadows.
She's huge like a spaceship.
Her eyes glow in the water.
Long tentacles fly like
ribbons behind her.
Silver-backed fish
scatter before her.

A wandering mother octopus
moves through the water.
Inside her body, she carries her eggs.
She looks for a den that is safe
and well hidden,
for a crack in a rock face or
a hole under a stone.

When octopuses need to move quickly,

they jet backward by sucking in seawater

and pumping it out through a funnel-like siphon.

An octopus sinks
like a huge
rubber flower.

Sand muddies the water
as she lands on
the seabed.

Octopuses use their tentacles like fingers to sense things.

They use the suckers on their tentacles to grip things.

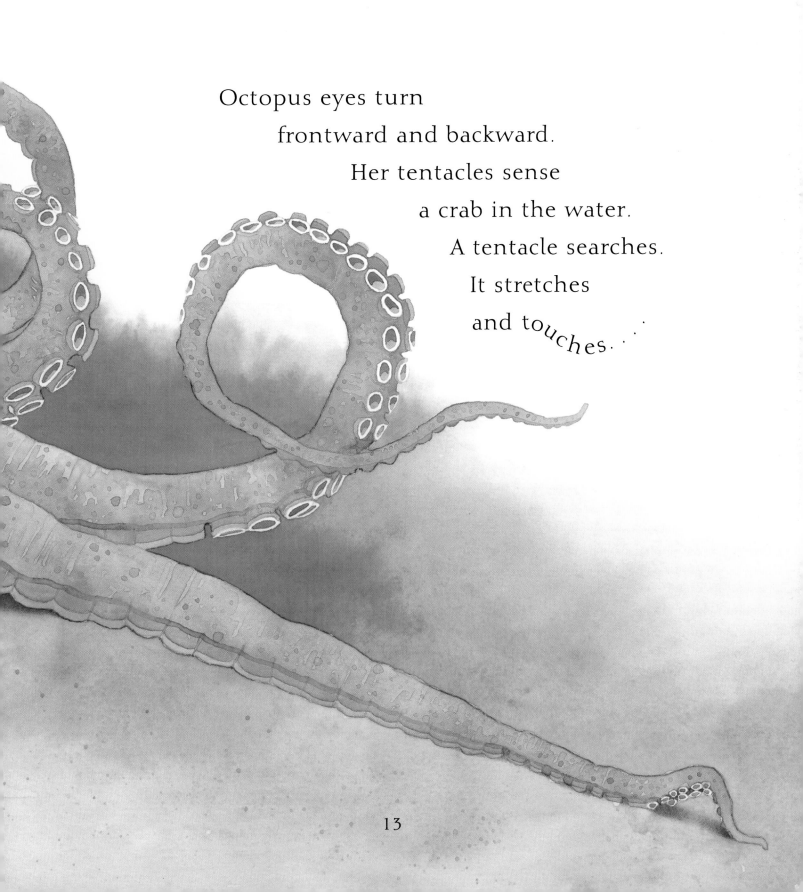

Octopus eyes turn
frontward and backward.
Her tentacles sense
a crab in the water.
A tentacle searches.
It stretches
and touches...

13

Unlucky
octopus!

14

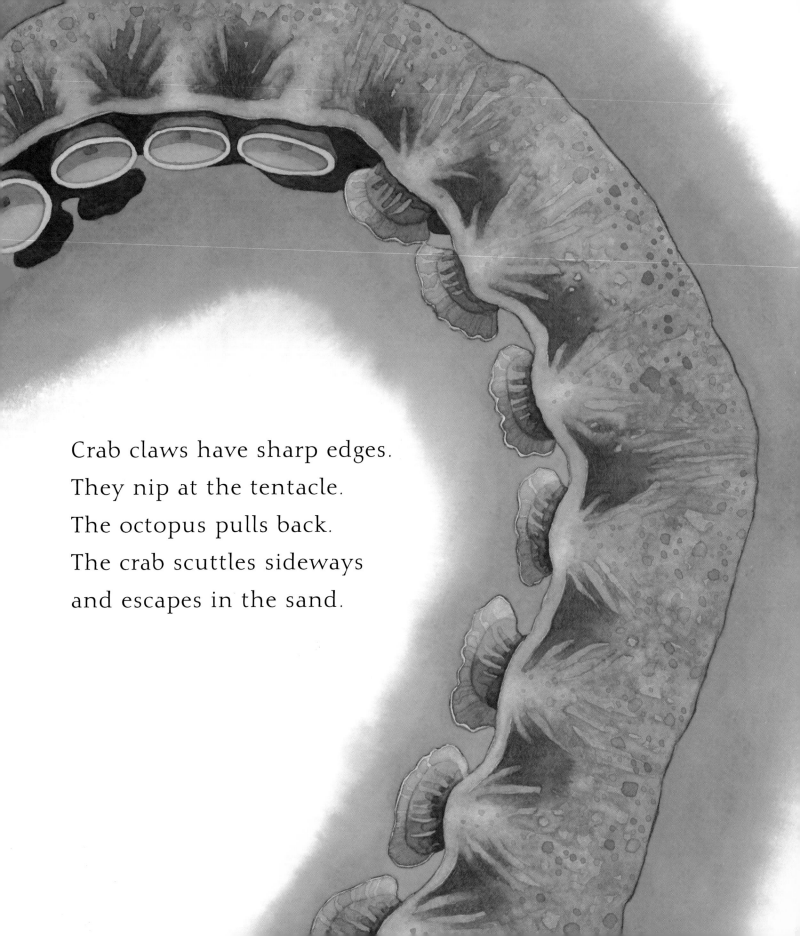

Crab claws have sharp edges.
They nip at the tentacle.
The octopus pulls back.
The crab scuttles sideways
and escapes in the sand.

A mother Giant octopus
slides over the seabed.
Her body stretches like taffy
over the stones.
Her skin ripples like seaweed.
She's black as the sea kelp.
The goggle-eyed octopus
feels her way forward.

Usually, the Giant octopus is reddish brown, but when it's hunting or hiding, it can change to become very dark or very pale within seconds.

17

But under a boulder,
a Wolf eel is waiting.
His mottled gray face darts
from the shadows.
His teeth strike
like daggers.
He rips off
a tentacle.

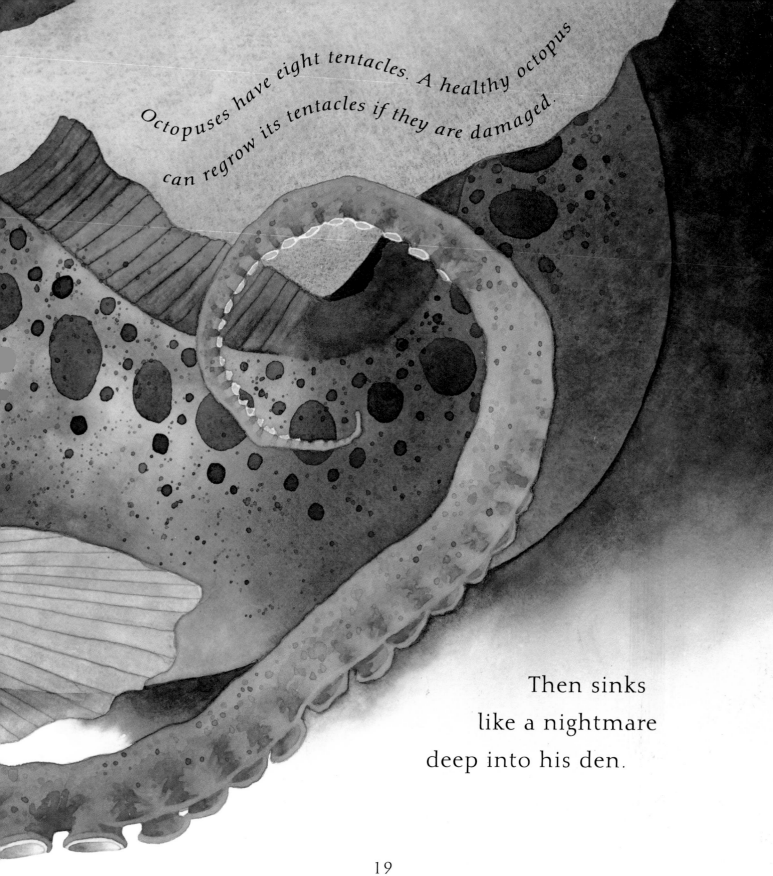

Octopuses have eight tentacles. A healthy octopus can regrow its tentacles if they are damaged.

Then sinks
like a nightmare
deep into his den.

19

If an octopus is attacked,
it will squirt out a cloud of inky liquid to hide its escape.

A frightened Giant octopus
squirts ink at the Wolf eel.
She shoots back from the boulder,
back over the seabed.
She's pumping and sucking
the sea from her body.

A quivering Giant octopus
rests on a boulder.

Underneath is a cave
that is easily guarded.

Octopuses are about as clever as cats—and like cats, they're very curious.

She squeezes inside.
She drags pebbles around her.

Her search for a home
is over at last.

Octopuses don't have any bones, and they can squeeze through the tiniest of holes.

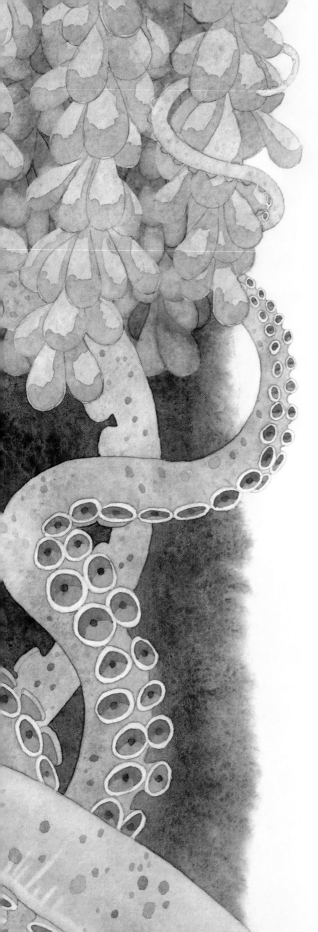

A mother Giant octopus lays
eggs in her cave den.
They hang from the roof
like grapes on a string.
She guards them from crabs
and nibbling fishes.
While her babies are growing,
she never eats and never rests.

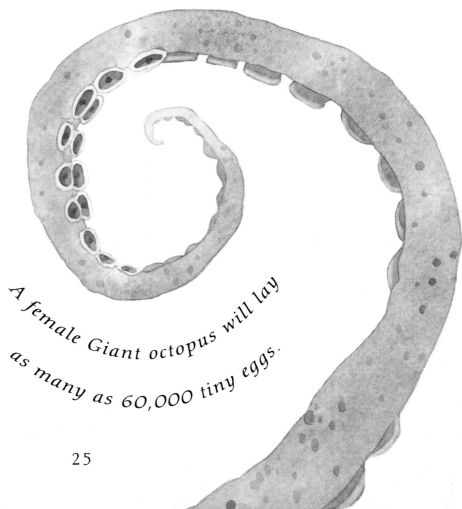

A female Giant octopus will lay
as many as 60,000 tiny eggs.

25

After five months, her babies
swim from their egg sacs.
They squirm and they wiggle.
They jet through the shadows.
They're sucking and pumping
the sea from their bodies.

Lots of other animals like to eat baby octopuses,
so only two or three out of every brood live to become adults.

A mother Giant octopus
rests in her cave den.
She watches her babies
swim up through
the water.

A gentle Giant octopus
shrinks in the shadows.
Her life is over as their lives begin.

Index

babies 25, 26, 27, 29

cleverness 22

color changing 16

den 8, 22–23

eggs 8, 25, 26

enemies 18, 20, 25

food 3

ink 20, 21

moving 6, 9, 21, 26

size 3

suckers 12

tentacles 6, 12, 13, 19

where Giant octopuses live 3

Look up the pages to find out
about all these octopus things.
Don't forget to look at both kinds
of words—this kind
and *this kind*.

KAREN WALLACE grew up in a log cabin in the woods of Quebec, Canada. Octopuses have always had a special place in her imagination, from the storybook monsters of folklore to the young octopus she watched escape from a fish trap, climb down a boat ladder, and sink back to the safety of the sea. Karen Wallace is the author of many picture books, including *Think of an Eel*, also illustrated by Mike Bostock, which won a Parents' Choice Award and the Kurt Maschler Award.

MIKE BOSTOCK, while illustrating this book, became fascinated by octopuses—the delicate changing color and texture of their skin, the rubbery, rippling way they move, and their transparent soap-bubble-like babies. Mike Bostock's other picture books include *Pond Year* by Kathryn Lasky, *A Song of Colors* by Judy Hindley, and the award-winning *Think of an Eel* by Karen Wallace.